Living Whole and Empowered

Presented by

Melissa C. Roberts, MS CPC

Perfect Time SHP Publishing

Copyright © 2021 **Melissa C. Roberts**

All rights reserved.

ISBN: 978-1-7347783-6-6

CONTENTS

CHAPTER ONE.. 2

Why Am I Here? Clearly Defining Your Divine Purpose

CHAPTER TWO 11

Living Tenaciously

CHAPTER THREE 20

Miscarried to Purpose Carried

CHAPTER FOUR.. 29

Learning From Rizpah: Do What You Can, use What You Have, Persist Until Change Happens

CHAPTER FIVE 40

Phenomenally Empowered to Birth Life, Visions, and Greatness

CHAPTER SIX 49

Getting Past Yourself

CHAPTER SEVEN 58

Count It All Joy

Melissa C. Roberts

"Truly your divine purpose and the reason you are on this earth is already inside of you."

-Melissa Roberts

— CHAPTER ONE —

Why Am I Here? Clearly Defining Your Divine Purpose

By Melissa C. Roberts, MS, CPC

I am sure you have asked yourself this question at some point in your life. As a matter of fact, I will go so far to say, if you are reading this, I'm 99.9% positive you have asked yourself this question. You may have asked yourself this question just yesterday or last week or maybe even last month. This question can haunt you if you allow it or it can catapult you in the direction of your divine purpose.

It is inevitable, in our make up as human beings, to want to know more than we know. I know some may say this couple gets a bad rap, but we are to learn from our history, right? It started with Adam and Eve in the Garden of Eden (Genesis, Chapter 2). We have always wanted to know more and sometimes as in the case of Adam and Eve, the extent we go to can create great harm or even change the entire trajectory of one's life and lineage. In this case, Adam and Eve had been given everything they could have possibly wanted and/or needed, yet there was still that desire of knowledge that only was supposed to be for God, they were talked into wanting to know more. That is not what this chapter is about. Although, you will find throughout this chapter, you will have to learn more about you and what your life experiences have given you that have or will connect you to your purpose for being.

Some say calling and others say purpose. I strongly believe, you can be called to a position or title or even a career, someone can call you to accomplish a certain task, however, your purpose chooses you. Your purpose was placed in you at the point of conception. Your purpose is something you were crafted specifically for and provided with the unique talents and abilities to nurture and begin using for your good and others. I believe your purpose is tied very closely to who you are. I remember as a little girl, I always told my parents that I wanted to be a lawyer when I grew up. I did not turn out to be a lawyer, but I am happy that I am an advocate. Thank goodness lawyer means advocate and an advocate can look different in many ways and can be walked out in many different facets. Truly your divine purpose and the reason you are on this earth is already inside of you. It is just a matter of you connecting with it and walking it out. Some may disagree with that statement "your purpose is placed in you from point of conception", and you were specifically and uniquely made based on your purpose to be fulfilled. A global poll done by The Gallup states that 85% of people in the world are unhappy with their job (https://news.gallup.com/). So that means only 15% of the people in the world enjoy what they do for a vocation or as a career. This is amazing and can answer a lot of questions when it comes to understanding the mental health challenges we face today. You must know that with the number of hours we spend at work, it can take a toll on one mentally if they are not happy or do not feel fulfilled in what they are doing 8 – 12 hours of the day. That is a sad statistic, and therefore it can be vitally important for you to be able to clearly identify your purpose and be encouraged to walk it out every day of your life and not waste another moment.

There are many reasons why people are not fulfilling their purpose. Someone may have told you "You can't or won't make enough money doing that" or "you don't have the right look" or "you are not the right shape or even color to be successful at that". The thing about your purpose, no one gets to tell you what your purpose is, but they may be able to confirm what is already inside of you. That might be a little confusing, so let me break it down for you this way. As you are going through life, you will find there will be things you like to do, or you find certain things bring you joy when you do them. You may find there are some things you find interesting or what you might call a "hobby". They, in most cases, are not your purposes, but maybe a calling in a particular season of your life. Your purpose is something that you do, and you flow in it. You find when you are operating in your divine purpose, time goes by so quickly without you thinking about it and it is something you will do even if there is no compensation associated with it. You feel fulfilled when it is complete, and you feel you have contributed something of value that is greater than yourself. If you allow yourself to dream again or give yourself permission to dream again, you begin to look at those things that bring you great joy while you are giving of yourself. There is something about fulfilling your purpose, you are in many ways always helping others.

How to Get Started Towards Fulfilling Your Purpose

To begin your journey on fulling your purpose, here are some things you can do to move you in the right direction and can get you started.

Accept your decision - you must give yourself permission to accept the fact that you are designed specifically to fulfill a divine purpose. We are generally accustomed to fulfilling the desires of the society we live in, but that will not always bring you joy or help you to satisfy the purpose within. Regardless of what friends and family say, you must be comfortable in the decision you have made and be prepared to walk it out.

Only tell a few – you must be careful when defining your purpose in who you share with because not everyone will support your decision or be happy for your fulfillment. So be very selective and trust only those who have proven themselves to be trustworthy. The idea is to manage your circle. Only provide the opportunity for positivity to flow as you are on your journey to greatness and success. Press in to clarify who you are and what you are looking to accomplish and how you will accomplish it. This is the time for you to become clearer, at least, with your circle, you can bounce ideas off your trustworthy counterparts.

Go full out – when I say "go full out" I mean to press in completely, that simply means, let all your positive energies flow in the direction of completing tasks and goals that will move you closer to your divine purpose. Remember, you will not feel like you are working because you will flow in the activity. However, you want to make sure you are *moving* in the right direction. Sometimes you can depend on your circle to remind you in those times you are feeling down, or you may feel like things aren't going the way you have anticipated. It is okay! I promise. Things will not always look the way you think they should but keep moving forward in discovering your divine purpose. Sometimes, it may take you adding to your circle, a professional Coach. Someone who can help you bring clarity to your thoughts and goals. Do that if that is what it will take for you to go full out!

Accept failures and mistakes – now there will be times where you will not see progression. As a matter of fact, you are going to fail or make mistakes and feel like you are standing still, don't stop - keep moving, keep doing, keep going. You may think you are not progressing, but if you are moving forward, you are progressing, learning, and growing. Every step is moving you closer to your purpose and learning more about who you are purposed to be.

This last one is very important to remember to do, ***Reflect and meditate*** – set aside time for you to reflect on where you have been and what you have learned. Setting aside a time to meditate quietly on what you are striving for, can provide you the opportunity to reflect and listen to your spirit for guidance and direction. You have exactly what you need inside to accomplish your goals in working in your divine purpose, so don't give up and don't use this time to tear yourself down or bring in negative thoughts. This time can only be effective if you use it wisely. Set aside a time and place. If you need to schedule it on your planner, do that to make sure it happens often.

It is your time to feel accomplished and successful in what you offer the world, so do what you were created to do!

About Melissa C. Roberts

Melissa C. Roberts is a certified Professional Life Coach. She has a Master's in the Studies in Human Behaviors and a Bachelor of Science in Criminal Justice.

She is currently the owner of a coaching and consultant practice, Living Whole, LLC, where the primary focus is mind, body, and soul living. Her coaching and consultant philosophy is partnership, integrity, transparency and enabling positive change through added value. Melissa is the founder of God's Whole Woman magazine, which encourages positive life choices for women.

Melissa resides in Griffin, Georgia with her husband, Stephen Roberts, III. They co-own a nonprofit organization, RunFast, Inc. which works to educate the community on good health practices through the competitive sport of Track. They have six adult children and two grandsons. She enjoys spending time with family, reading and adding value to the lives of others.

Ella Flemister

"You are created with the ability to recover from adversity"

- Ella Flemister

— CHAPTER TWO —

Living Tenaciously

By Ella Flemister, LMFT

What does it mean to live tenaciously? Tenacious defined by Merriam-Webster: Persistent in existence and not easily pulled apart. You all have struggles, and some tear at your very soul, but you don't have to be destroyed by your circumstances. You are created with the ability to recover from adversity. A renewed self-image can emerge time after time when you embrace an awareness of the need to build *mental muscles*. This is vital to one's ability to become resilient and is foundational for tenacious living.

Your core values, purpose and knowing you have the ability to recover can help you maintain the momentum needed for your journey. So, prepare yourself for road blocks and disappointment. When you find yourself in the valley of doubt, say, "This is not my forever."

Know that you don't need everyone on your team to accomplish whatever you aspire to do. To start, you need a strong desire and a reason why. There is a need to counteract thoughts that creep in and cause you to doubt your abilities, being mindful of with whom and where you share your dreams. Not everyone will cheer you on because not all have the ability to be happy for and bless others. During those times when you feel desolate, remind yourself that these feelings are pure emotions, not based on facts. Don't trap yourself with distorted thinking that may well be rooted in childhood experiences. Please remember, when people you depend on walk away, they were not yours anyway.

When you make a mistake, tap into that resilient part of you and keep moving. Be aware, mistakes are necessary so you may learn what not to do further down the road and upon arrival. They are indispensable must-haves that slow you down, cause you to rest, help you to reimagine, redesign, and remember the importance of a stable foundation for any endeavor. You can't willy-nilly your way to anything that will eventually have substance. Dr. Tony Evans said it beautifully, "Foundations aren't pretty, but they better be solid."

Finding yourself in difficult situations, your initial response is likely to be that of confusion, disappointment, fear, anger etc. You may even get stuck and struggle with the idea of there actually being a solution to your dilemma. However, when you are fully aware of and envision situations as temporary states, you don't lose hope. Sometimes you need a shoulder to cry on but not just any shoulder. Therefore, building solid relationships that can serve as safety nets can help you emerge from the darkness with renewed hope. Think about times when you were at a low state, and someone gave you a simple hug. It probably felt good just being touched by another in the moment. But there is more to the story. That good feeling from a hug only lasts a little while.

An honest assessment of self is essential in maintaining balanced mental health. If yours is at risk, a mental health professional can provide you with a safe space to bare your soul. In choosing a professional, you should feel at ease in the session, meaning you are connecting.

In my professional setting, I utilize information from family history to aid in the therapy process. People are often uplifted and freed from emotional chains just by coming into realization of how mannerisms have been passed down to them. Family history marked by psychological, sexual and physical abuse, infidelity and violence can cause emotional trauma that stunts personal growth of those who lived through it. As stated before, you are resilient and you can recover from abuse. You don't have to just "float" through life. God has equipped you with the ability to recover from childhood adversity and abuse. But there is the need to silence the shame associated with the traumatic experiences.

There is a direct correlation between how you think and how you experience life. If you want greater enjoyment in life, free up mind space that is now occupied by thoughts that trouble you. Change your narrative to something more to your liking. In times of difficulty, remind yourself **"This is not my forever."**

Don't allow yourself to become imprisoned by the behavior of others. When you are treated wrong, recognize the person is dealing with personal issues that most likely have nothing to do with you. Scripture tells us to be at peace with all men as much as is humanly possible. You don't have the ability to change anyone. Making changes in one's own life take determination. You may embody peacefulness and are challenged anyway. It is ok to no longer allow someone in your space if they are antagonizing you. Getting into an argument with them would be fruitless, even though you might feel as if you "really" got them told. When you are angry, you can't make sound decisions. This applies to everyone.

Family can be so misguided that they may feel they have a right to mistreat you. Know this is a complete lie. Maintaining your peace is essential to good mental health. God never intended for us to be a doormat for anyone. So, family do not get a pass here. Be kind to yourself when others won't.

Experiencing loss takes a lot out of you. However, along this journey lies the opportunity for developing a mindset that allows you to live life to the fullest. When you really understand just how precious the gift of life is, you can and will want to do life with tenacity. No matter what your circumstances are, you really need to get as much out of life as possible. Pricilla Shirer explained it like this, "If you think you are young because of your age, and you only have until 30 before you die, you are old. If you are 50 and will live until 100, you are young." This is reason enough to pursue life purposely and with tenacity.

My husband and I took my mother (deceased now), on her first plane trip. Flying from Georgia to Dallas, everything was going quite well until we hit some of the scariest turbulence I have experienced. The flight attendant has just passed out sandwiches. It was clear that momma was a little shaken. In his effort to lighten the moment, my husband (in his own unique manner), said, "Moa, you might ought to eat that sandwich, it might be your last one." Momma's initial response was, or at least looked like "What did this fool just say?!". Then she laughed and we all laughed, and soon it was all calm again. She let go of her fear of flying and created beautiful memories. You don't know when your journey on earth will end, so it is imperative for you to do your best to get as much as possible out of life today. Not everyone has the ability to travel, and do everything desired in this life. But you can carve out something. **Don't measure your happiness against the experiences of others.**

Most people want to be a part of something. Good health is promoted by being in the company of others. The pandemic was a good demonstration of this basic need. However, it is never good to compromise your integrity, or lower your standards just to be accepted by anyone. Too often people do this and are left feeling less than. One the flip side, what is there to gain from being a stand-alone Diva? Consider this: If someone is wearing the same outfit as another, one or both might get ticked off and ditch theirs. An alternate approach might be to say, "Looks nice on you!" **Be kind to other women.**

We all have what are called turning points in life where decisions are made that change lives forever. I'll share some of mine.

Age 16 – Abandoned all plans to further my education. Dropped out of high school with all A's. (I don't recommend this)!

Age 17 – Fell in love and married a sailor. First born at age 18. Gave birth to two more.

Age 30 – Diagnosed with cancer (stage 4). This was first in a series of serious health issues over the years. Health returned completely.

Age 36 – Earned my GED!

Age 51 – Pursued a degree in psychology which ultimately paved the way for the work I love today.

Age 59 – Earned a Master's Degree in Marriage and Family Therapy.

It is never too late to start living life tenaciously. Purpose in your heart to do so. Take care of yourself first. There is nothing selfish about this. If your mental or physical health is at stake, take a step back and rethink your situation. Remember you can't fully be available for others if you are not taking care of you.

About Ella Flemister, LMFT

Ella Flemister, LMFT (Licensed Marriage and Family Therapist) is the owner of Tenacious Life Therapy, LLC and resides in Griffin, GA. She is also an independent contractor, providing on-line therapy to clients residing in the state of Georgia.

Ella's vision is to utilize her training in a manner that will benefit families, couples, individuals and communities. She is also wholeheartedly dedicated to educating clients about loss resulting from dementia.

Ella earned a Bachelor of Science (BS) Degree from Clayton State University in Psychology and Human Services and a Master of Family Therapy (MFT), from Mercer University School of Medicine, Macon GA. She is a Certified Dementia Care Specialist (CDCS) from Evergreen Certifications and holds a Professional Certificate of Gerontology from Clayton State University.

Ella is married to her husband of 49 years and is the proud mother of three, grandmother of four and one great granddaughter!

Hilari Seagears

"God can do ANYTHING!"

- Hilari Seagears

— CHAPTER THREE —

Miscarried to Purpose Carried

By Hilari Seagears

Surrendered. Fulfilled. Whole. I hear these words and immediately consider James 1:1, *Count it all joy when you meet various trials. Know that the testing of your faith produces steadfastness. Let it have its full effect, that you may be perfect and complete, lacking in nothing.* This New Testament scripture embodies the concept of living whole – God's way – the best way. There is beauty in pain.

Being raised in a household with two extremely loving and spirit filled parents is what established me. My pride and joy used to always be my enormously gifted and talented family, especially as this secular society continues to dilute the original intent and dynamic of family. My siblings and I were raised serving in church with Jesus and music securing our family bond. My parents were the epitome of the example to be fruitful and multiply. As my sisters and I grew older, and everyone started getting married it seemed the next best thing to do was have children and my siblings did that well. They were definitely following in my parent's footsteps! When it was my turn, my husband and I immediately noticed that we struggled with fertility. For over a year we could not conceive. When we finally did, our pregnancy did not look like everyone else's. It had nothing to do with him. It had nothing to do with me. It had *everything* to do with LIFE. Unfortunate circumstances caused us to enter some of our darkest days yet, and I wasn't ready.

My biggest trial in life has been dealing with miscarriage. My first one was challenging because it took four months for the baby to pass through my body. My second was challenging because we lost the baby on Christmas Day, moments after sharing the news. My third was challenging because I ended up having a surgery that made my "issues" worse. Through it all, I had to fight through pain, doubt, and shame. I learned that God doesn't allow challenges to beat us down or taunt us. Rather, He desires that we bring our brokenness to Him so that we may experience *His* transformational power. God can do ANYTHING! The Lord extended grace for me to work through each loss so I could gain strength to overcome. Eventually I would be in a position to help others do the same. I quickly learned that through pain, your purpose can be revealed.

Death left me broken in my mind, body, heart and spirit. I was a senior in high school when my father died. Just after being married, I lost six close family members in less than two years. Grief has tried to suffocate me...BUT GOD! *HE* saved me from depression, fear, anger and more. I was desperate for healing and God took me on a journey to develop unshakable faith and unbreakable trust in *Him*. Because I learned to trust His character, I knew to trust His judgements. Whatever tests challenge my ability to live whole, I consider the purpose it carries so I can glorify God through my pain. It would be selfish and irresponsible of me to keep this revelation to myself. *Any*one who experiences grief can recover. You just have to feel, deal, heal, and reveal!

Wholeness is not a thing you can get or obtain. Wholeness is a person. Wholeness is God! When we receive Jesus and His salvation, *then* we are complete. Don't get me wrong. You can know Christ and still be broken. Yet, boast in your weakness – that's scriptural! 2 Corinthians 12:9-10 declares, *My grace is sufficient, my power is made perfect in weakness. Therefore, I will gladly boast about my weaknesses, so Christ's power may rest on me. That's why, for Christ's sake, I delight in weaknesses, insults, hardships, persecutions, and difficulties. For when I am weak, then I am strong.* Jesus is true strength. When there is chaos, He brings peace. When you are hurting, He provides His Word. That empowerment alone leads to a relationship with wholeness.

My miscarriages caused a breaking point. Emotionally, I was too unstable to process anything. I knew that if I did not pursue help, my brokenness would consume me and that would affect more people than just me. I owed it to God, my family and myself to grieve *His* way. If I could overcome the trials in my life, God would allow opportunities for me to minister to the brokenhearted. My recovery was bigger than me!

Let this simple yet necessary process revive the dead places in your life so you can help save someone else. First, you have to feel. This takes patience and a certain degree of maturity. God gifted everyone with feelings. They serve a permanent purpose that allows us to experience abundant life. When circumstances influence our temperaments, it is pertinent to not adopt extremes. For instance, pregnancy/infant loss will cause serious trauma. Choosing to cope with immense grief using substances, toxic relationships, and others like this will only produce temporary pleasure to an eternal tragedy. Choosing to do the exact opposite – nothing – can be just as detrimental. Harbored feelings will manifest and fester in numerous ways. Eventually you will get to a place where you find yourself lashing out, adopting addictions, or catering to spirits of darkness that weren't meant to have purpose. When I greeted my raw emotions, they were heavy! So, I released them to God in prayer. I wept, screamed, and cried out from my spirit. God met me in perfect timing and with perfect peace. The more I embraced His grace, my heart was able to *begin* to truly heal.

The next part of this process is to deal. Give yourself reasonable time to recognize and label each emotion. It is not healthy to simply dwell on unpleasant thoughts and feelings. Doing so invites the manifestation of anxiety. Remember, grief is a battle of the mind, body *and* spirit. Even when you feel grounded in your soul, it is just as necessary to pay attention to your mental state. Healing and deliverance are not synonymous here. For a barren woman, the Lord can open up your womb, yet your mind still be bound. Whatever the stronghold, you have to call it out and cancel it. *That* is how you deal with darkness. When you are tempted to believe you will never be able to have children, you speak Matthew 19:26 from your heart declaring, "With

God all things are possible". When it seems all your relationships are failing and you are at odds with loved ones, find your quiet space with the Lord and recall Exodus 14:14 that encourages, "The Lord will fight for you, you need only to be still". Affirmations will be fuel to your brokenness, but there is no combination of words more powerful and transformational than God's Word.

As you begin to deal with each avenue of your grief, you will surely feel relief from the weight of life. *That* is healing! Sometimes, we pray for miracles and then don't know how to act when they actually happen. Or rather, we're surprised that God came through and provided what we needed (not wanted) in that circumstance. True healing is when you operate in a peculiar state of mind. That means, although the doctor looks at you and says you are just a case of bad luck and there is no certainty that you will ever have children, you can find courage in your soul to have faith and believe God can and will do exceedingly and abundantly above what we could ever ask of Him! Operate in your healing as if the miracle is already sitting in your lap. One of my closest friends always encourages me that my fight is already fixed. Jesus has overcome the entire world. Whatever giant you are facing, The Lord is greater than it! Finances tight? Jesus is *thee* provider. Lost a loved one? Jesus is our peace. Struggling with your identity? Jesus declares you are fearfully and wonderfully made. You already have the victory over your brokenness.

When you accept Jesus into your heart, you invite wholeness into your life. Grab hold of that *truth*, experience it, live it, and then go tell somebody else. Reveal it! We were made to be reproducing disciples. The point of your victory is not to keep it to yourself. The most impactful decision you can make is to share the faithfulness and Gospel of Jesus Christ everywhere you go. Your personal healing toward wholeness is bigger than just you. Could it be that your journey was intended to save someone else on theirs?

If you receive nothing else from these words, remember to seek God with your entire being. He is the only solution to the fulfilment and satisfaction of living whole. Erase all pressure to be perfect and "have it all together" and replace it with Jesus. Grief is hard. Grief is unpredictable. Grief is inconsiderate. But God is faithful. God is patient. God is wholeness.

About Hilari Seagears

A God-fearing disciple, wife to Bobby Seagears, mother to Angel, Jordan, and Christian-Noel (in heaven), author, and more. Born and raised in Gaithersburg, Maryland, Hilari is the eighth of twelve children. She values relationships with God, family and friends. While she is initially shy and reserved, her tested 94percent introvert-ness only lasts for a moment because she loves to laugh and enjoy life. As Hilari began to experience what seemed like a never-ending cycle of loss, beginning with the passing of her father, her faith remained anchored in God. Eventually, she would have three consecutive miscarriages that left her feeling shattered. Through a spirit of resilience Hilari was determined to rise above her circumstances. Her current passion is to encourage the hearts of those who feel stuck in their misery. Her ministry, BOLD Resilience LLC, serves those hurting as she unapologetically carries the truth and heart of Christ everywhere she goes.

Jennifer Creswell

"Empowered Women Use What They Have"

-Jennifer Creswell

— CHAPTER FOUR —

Learning From Rizpah: Do What You Can, use What You Have, Persist Until Change Happens

By Jennifer Creswell

I love stories, especially if the stories feature an "underdog" standing up to injustice, especially if those stories are true. Historically speaking, women have often found themselves in a position of very little power and very much distress. Discussing the reasons for this reality are outside the scope of this offering, however, to this day, it is commonplace to find ourselves or sisters confronting seemingly insurmountable difficulties which have been handed to them out of no fault of their own.

A story just like this is told in the Bible, it is the story of a woman named Rizpah. Being a child of a preacher man – I was schooled in scripture from the earliest age. However, this particular story is one that was never featured in the nighttime *Bible Stories for Children* book, perhaps because it is a gruesome tale.

Rizpah was a concubine of King Saul. Dress it up how you wish, but a concubine is not the same as a wife. In Old Testament terms a "concubine" had zero rights and one main purpose. According to Easton's Bible Dictionary a concubine *"had no authority in the family, nor could they share in the household government."*

The *Dictionary of Bible Themes* explains it this way: *"A woman, often a servant or slave, with whom a man had regular sexual relations, but to whom he was not married. A concubine did not have the rights of a wife and her children were not rightful heirs, though a wife might offer a servant to her husband as a concubine to have children on her behalf."*[1]

And right here, there begs to be a discussion of what exactly was the benefit of this relationship on the woman's side. I am sure a look at ancient history would remind us that in the context of this biblical age, a woman without a man was a poor and destitute woman, and I imagine being

---

[1]

somebody's concubine was superior to being left to forage for a living as a prostitute.

Regardless, establish this: Rizpah was a concubine of King Saul. Perhaps being a King's concubine was a little superior to being a regular man's concubine – still the duties and rights remained the same. The account of 2 Samuel reveals that Saul is dead, his dynasty ended and King David is now in power, what Rizpah has left is her two sons, Armoni and Mephibosheth. Somehow, the lives of Rizpah's sons along with five others of Saul's offspring, are bargained off by King David as a way to right the wrongs of the previous administration. The exact reasoning is much more complex, but the result is simple: Rizpah's sons plus five others are handed over to be killed. The Bible describes their deaths this way: (2 Samuel 21:9) *"The men of Gibeon executed them on the mountain before the L*^{ORD}*. So, all seven of them died together at the beginning of the barley harvest."* Execution is a very clinical description of what happened to these men. Scholars say they were "impaled on stakes" and Scripture says their bodies were left there. Bodies, killed by impalement, left to rot, left to be picked at by scavengers, left to be seen and talked about by passersby. Nameless bodies, impaled on a hillside, the bodies of a lowly concubine, offered no funeral, no memorial service, no proper burial, just bodies left to bake, decay and eventually rot in the sunshine.

There are so many unanswered questions in this story. Did Rizpah watch her sons die? Did Rizpah beg for mercy on their behalf? Did she try to send a message to the King? Did she know beforehand what was getting ready to take place? Did she have a chance to say some final words to her boys? Frustratingly, we do not know, in fact Scripture gives no record of any words spoken by Rizpah. We do know, however, what Rizpah did.

"Then Rizpah ... spread burlap on a rock and stayed there the entire harvest season. She prevented the scavenger birds from tearing at their bodies during the day and stopped wild animals from eating them at night." (2 Samuel 21:10 NLT)

She spread burlap on a rock. She stayed there for the entire harvest season (probably about six months). During the day she fought off scavenger birds, and at night she faced down the wild animals looking for a snack. The sad story resolves by informing us that her actions were reported to King David and in the end, the bodies were collected and given a proper burial.

Rizpah, a concubine, a "secondary wife", a silent figure who must stand helplessly and watch her sons slaughtered is still remembered today, not as powerless but as powerful. How did this wordless woman find her way into scripture? Rizpah without fanfare, without a media team, without personal connections to the people in power, determined her own response to ugly circumstances, and in doing so, this woman who many would have labeled as "powerless" showed amazing power. What can we learn from Rizpah? How can we too respond to ugly circumstances in such a way that we are not powerless, but powerful? Perhaps the following observations will help us:

1. **Rizpah used the desperation of her situation to provoke her to action: EMPOWERED WOMEN DO WHAT THEY CAN**. A common response to Rizpah's situation would easily be to lay on a victim's couch and cry, to drown in memories, to sit and wish for a different outcome, and certainly no one would have blamed her for doing so. But Rizpah chose instead to channel the sorrow and heartache of the moment into action. She left her home and went to the ground zero of her heartache, focusing the fury of her sorrow into fighting off the birds of prey and wild animals. Make no mistake, we humans all have one thing in common – many are the circumstances and situations out of our control – but we all possess the ability to choose our

response – no matter how devastating the situation. Rizpah chose to act. We also can choose to act. We do not remember Rosa Parks' words, but no one will ever forget her action, she sat down. History is made by people who act, not necessarily speak. Even when faced with the most difficult situations, we can choose action instead of passivity.

2. **Rizpah used what she had to effect change. EMPOWERED WOMEN USE WHAT THEY HAVE.** I imagine Rizpah felt so acutely her "lack" in the moment of her sons' capture: lack of connections, lack of finances, lack of power. A byproduct of an unexpected crisis is usually a quick assessment of one's resources and depending upon the magnitude of the crisis – a quick realization of how much money, power, or connections one is missing. Generally speaking, what ensues is the "if only" game humanity loves to play: "if only I had more money", "if only I knew someone", "if only I had a better education" etc. Did Rizpah entertain these thoughts? We do not know. But we do know that in the end, she took what she had, a piece of burlap and headed to lay it out on a rock close to her son's now impaled corpses. Burlap, the most

rudimentary and common of fabrics. A fabric common to the poor, a fabric which biblically speaking is symbolic of mourning, humility and poverty. Rizpah didn't take a tent, animal skins, a pot for cooking, she took what she had on hand, in the house, at her disposal: common, plain burlap. Empowered women use what they have. Mother Teresa's early days were spent walking the slums of Calcutta and sitting with the dying, washing the sores of the poor, teaching the children, without financial backing, without doctors or helpers, without medicines or supplies, she alone would leave her convent in the morning and spend the days walking the slums with what she had, *"the heart of Jesus"* to serve *"the unwanted, the unloved, the uncared for."* Empowered women use what they have.

3. **Rizpah kept her vigil until something changed: EMPOWERED WOMEN PERSIST UNTIL SOMETHING CHANGES.** Bringing her sons' back to life was not possible, but regaining their honor, provoking a decent burial, was Rizpah's heart cry. Scripture tells us she stayed from the early harvest until the latter rains – by conservative estimates, biblical scholars say this was a period of

six months. Rizpah spent six months outside in the elements, day and night, guarding, facing scavenging animals, protesting, making a statement. What was she thinking as days turned into weeks, and then months? One day, King David sent his men to gather the bones and Rizpah's vigil came to an end, her purpose now accomplished. Empowered women do not give up easily, facing difficulty with determination, they stand and wait, they guard and wait, they protest and wait until at last change comes.

Rizpah – what a woman. Her heartbreaking story could well have ended at the point of her sons' death. Instead, Rizpah chose to act, using what she had, and persisting until change happened. What situation are you faced with today? What heartbreaking difficulty has found your home address? I challenge you to resist the urge to sit on the couch and assess your inadequacies wishing for change. Instead, grab what you do have, and do something until change comes, because that's what empowered women do.

Citations

(Easton, M. G. (n.d.). *Reference List - Concubine*. King James Bible Dictionary.
http://www.kingjamesbibledictionary.com/Dictionary/concubine.)

About Jennifer Creswell

Jennifer is passionate about Jesus, chocolate, and all things pink. Having been rescued by Jesus, from brokenness and confusion at age 25, she is determined to spend the rest of her life proclaiming the freedom found in Christ and the transforming power of the Word of God.

Jennifer has spent years teaching on a multi-generational level, including high school Bible Class, weekly Bible Study and regularly preaching at her home church.

Jen and her husband Scott serve as part of the Executive Pastoral Team at Griffin First Assembly. The product of missionary parents, her spiritual roots run deep, as well as her fluency in Spanish, love for spicy food and outstanding appreciation for hot water.

Pastor Gwennette Watson

"I had to sit still and let God work his plan."

- Pastor Gwennette Watson

— CHAPTER FIVE —

Phenomenally Empowered to Birth Life, Visions, and Greatness

By Pastor Gwennette Watson

"Now you understand, just why my head's not bowed. I don't shout or jump about or have to talk real loud. … 'Cause I'm a woman, phenomenally, phenomenal woman, that's me". As extracted from Maya Angelou's poem "Phenomenal Woman" these words eloquently express the essence of God's creation known as the woman. Women were created with the innate abilities to create life, nurture, and console. Also, we have been appointed to organize, lead, and grow whatever our hands touch. Since biblical times, women have been called to lead and not only be in subservient roles.

I want to take a moment to simply encourage women who may be having feelings of inferiority, whether it's on your job, in your home, or even in ministry. No matter how inferior others may see you, you are significant in the roles you were called to because you were divinely anointed for a purpose that far exceeds any limitations anyone may try to place on you.

Sometimes we lose our sense of purpose because of past experiences and other traumatic encounters that come and get us distracted and off track. But as we realign our self-inflicted purpose with God's divine assignment, living life in abundance will prevail.

Jeremiah 1:5 (NKJV) states, "Before I formed you in the womb I knew you; before you were born I sanctified you; I ordained you a prophet to the nations". I decree and declare that every hang up that you have had in your life was purposed for your destiny. You can go ahead and serve the devil notice that "I have purpose in my life and I WILL FULFILL IT. This is the time to trust your deepest desires and exercise your faith as you execute all you can conceive in your mind. Your thoughts and dreams aren't by happenstance, they were planted and await you to nurture and expand them the way God intended.

Allow me to share two references of women who didn't just "talk the talk", but they walked in purpose with boldness in spite of adversity and challenges.

The Story of Phoebe

I remember reading in Romans 16: 1-2 about Phoebe and her role as a deacon. We hear a lot of subservient roles women played in biblical times, but possibly not a lot about those in leadership. Allow me to jumpstart your research on others. What we do know is her appointment as a deacon meant she not only gained the trust of many, but they also valued her as divinely anointed to carry-out the duties. In other words, she put in the work and the WORK validated her abilities.

In the scripture, Phoebe was on her way to Rome to take Paul's letter to the Romans. The interesting thing is that there were indeed other means Paul could have utilized to get the letter to them; but when the opportunity came, Phoebe spoke when no one else wanted to, and Paul honored her request. Not because he didn't have other options but because he knew he could trust her to do the work and lead the people in ministry as God intended. Paul sent an advance recommendation of this sister in Christ so the Romans will receive her and support her during her stay in their city. Scripture further tells us of Paul's thoughts on the woman's role that some would say are controversial or contradictory to his support of Phoebe to carry-out this task, but he makes it clear that Phoebe has some recognized standing within the church. In other words, Paul knew the value of what women could do in serving the church. One of the greatest traits of a leader is one who is willing to work alongside the people and get in the trenches to get the job done, not just use their leadership role to dictate and give orders.

The Story of Gwennette Watson

My husband passed away April 14, 2018 and by that time I had served as co-pastor for 19 years. His transition didn't give me much time to rethink ministry, I immediately stepped up as the Senior Pastor. Just as Phoebe stepped up when Paul needed someone to deliver the letter to the Romans, I gave God another yes and accepted the challenge because I knew He was speaking to me concerning elevating to the pastoral role. I had watched my husband and sat under his teaching for all those years only to later realize that I was getting on the job training. I knew I had my work cut out for me, not because ministry was new to me, but because the people were used to my husband's teaching and he was a male.

However, the 19+ years of ministry trained and prepared me for the present day. Even before my husband became a minister, he would be traveling and singing on programs and funerals. God divinely put us together. I was never the one seeking to be in the forefront, I was shy, and stayed away from the spotlight. I simply backed and supported my husband, my Pastor, no matter what and I became comfortable in that. In the days of his illness, he would be pushing me with little things. He didn't force me out there, but in the latter times it would be small things he did to build me up and equip me for what divine order had already ordained. As time progressed, he would ask me to step-up and do things to assist with ministry. Ministry starts at home first. I don't think I would be able to stand in ministry like I am now if it wasn't for the training and the life he exemplified. He lived what he preached and it was a blessing to witness it firsthand while also giving me the encouragement I needed, not realizing what I was being prepared for.

My identity was merged into the commitment and devotion to my husband. Although I achieved plenty, because he encouraged and supported me during our marriage, it wasn't until his transition that I realized I had not fully lived my best part of loving Me. This was not from a spirit of selfishness and neglect, my husband took great care of me and ensured I had experiences to travel, minister, and care after those that mean the world to me. However, that was our life, joined as one. In this process, I had to administer a self-evaluation to determine if my life was to dwell in the grave with my husband or if it is to be resurrected and move into my God-given purpose. I realized that I didn't get to be favored with this length of time with such an anointed and powerful Man of God and that same power does not also rest within me. It resided dormant deep within and even in my moments of not knowing what the next step would be, God reached down and guided me to my rightful place. You see, Gwennette had to connect with Anthony at the football game, and it wasn't my time to do a lot of talking then, I had to sit still and let God work his plan. I didn't have to fight for the microphone and podium time, I just had to support and cover the movement as God intended and allow God to impart in me everything I needed. Upon my husband's transition, I could have easily sat still, but that's when God stepped in and was like, "No Daughter, NOW is the time for you to activate and execute…you have been graced, trained, and called for this very moment… NOW is the time I need you to be bold and audible and declare deliverance and healing upon my people."

Be Phenomenally You

The beauty of all this is the fact that in the last two illustrations, you see women who served in what our patriarchal society would consider as men's roles, but neither relinquished or had to compromise their femininity of being a woman to walk in leadership. Being a woman is a privilege that many don't get, but being divinely anointed for the various roles we often have to fulfill doesn't mean we have to portray being a man to fit in. Our super powers allow us to lead, or co-lead in some instances, and still be a woman…even with our bold confidence, quick wit, strategic decision making, strong work ethic, and multi-tasking selves. It's not a competition when you have been favored for the position, you just have to make sure your mindset understands the assignment and be ready to execute.

Therefore, I leave with you these words:

You ARE fearfully and wonderfully made;
You were created for a purpose and Chosen;
You were validated and qualified when you gave God your Yes;
You ARE the answer to someone's problem; AND
You are exactly who God called you to be, if you are being obedient to his word.

Go in grace and be great.

About Pastor Gwennette Watson

Pastor Gwennette B. Watson was born in Fulton County, graduated from Henry County High School, Flint River Technical College, and Mercer University

Since 1999, Pastor Watson served and toiled alongside her husband and Pastor, Apostle Anthony L. Watson, Sr., as the Co-Founder/Co-Pastor of New Faith Mission Non-Denominational Church, Inc. She accepted her call to preach the unadulterated gospel of Jesus Christ in February of 2002. After her husband's transition in April 2018, Pastor Watson moved as God instructed and redirected her strength to continue the legacy as Senior Pastor and is affectionately known as "Pastor G". Pastor G is currently working ministry full-time and released her debut book, Until Death Do Us Part, in 2019.

She resides in McDonough, GA and is a devoted mother to three beautiful children Mykeia (Mya), Keiashuna (Keekee), and Anthony Jr. (AJ).

Sandra Rawlings, MS, LPC, CPCS

"Stop comparing yourself to other women or their accomplishments"

- S. Rawlings

— CHAPTER SIX —

Getting Past Yourself

By Sandra Rawlings, MS, LPC, CPCS

We are women and proud of it! Women have come a long way in our abilities and strengths of what we can do to help contribute to ourselves, our families and our communities. We have excelled past the limitations that were put upon women in the past. So what is keeping you from fulfilling your dreams? What are the hurdles preventing you from the life God has designed for you to have?

Let's talk about some ideas which may be keeping you back from your destiny. I have heard it said that you are your own worst enemy. Those obstacles holding you back may be coming from within you.

First, how do you view yourself? What abilities do you have to share with the world? You think, "Am I smart enough, cute enough, have the right connections? Why bother? I could never be as good as other women. I am too shy, and don't have what it takes." **Stop comparing yourself to other women or their accomplishments.** God has given each of us our own individual, unique talents and abilities. Being different is ok. Being different does not mean we are wrong. We are not called to be the same, and how boring would that be if we were. No one is perfect and each of us have made our own share of mistakes.

Know what your talents are. Be aware of your limitations, and continue to learn to become better. It takes time and work. If you know of someone (whether in person or an authority or expert on the subject) who is doing what you would like, observe or talk with the person if you can. Learn from them. I would guess they have been practicing and learning as well.

Social Media has been a blessing for connection and observation, as it is providing a platform for us to see other people first hand. We can peer into the lives of others without having to leave our homes. It is a natural response to compare ourselves with them and what they are doing. We all want acceptance. Social Media has become so popular, some women and men are called "Influencers", as so many are watching what they post. They can actually influence their followers with buying habits and actions. How many let their emotions be persuaded by the number of "likes" they get? This can cause a comparison, and really play a part into our emotional wellbeing. Television and the internet can project a version of what and how we may think life should be, and how you view yourself. Be aware and guard what you see, as it will influence your thoughts.

That leads to the second area that could be keeping you from your success. **Be aware of your thinking, especially negative thinking.** Some may call it stinking thinking. It happens so fast and occurs so naturally every single day. Our self talk is what we are thinking and telling ourselves in our head, which can be positive or negative automatic thoughts. According to the National Science Foundation the average person has about 12,000 to 60,000 thoughts per day. Of those, 80 percent are **negative.** The majority of us may not be aware that we are thinking.

Have you ever had an idea, and you think to yourself, "This is great! This may be the very thing to help our lives be so much easier." It could be an idea you have for work or one for your home. It may be something that you have noticed as a need at church or for a friend.

I remember when my kids were younger, I needed some assistance with babysitting, yet I could not find a source to help me secure my sitter. One day, I was watching a movie with my daughter, "The Baby-Sitters Club" and thought to myself, "Yes! Something similar would be great, not only for us, but for other families with younger children." The young adults who could assist with this would also benefit by making some extra money while they are in high school or college. Sounded like a good idea, yet just thinking about the obstacles that could potentially cause issues, such as transportation or liability, deflated that dream, and it soon faded. It led to more negative thoughts "that was a dumb idea, no one would want it anyway." "What makes me think that I could start something?"

When you doubt yourself by listening to your negative self talk, it will hold you back from the actions to take you forward. Self doubt from your thoughts can lead to anxiety and depression. "I don't feel good enough." I doubt that my skills are useful to anyone." Again, we are made for relationships with others. Feeling less-than will challenge your desire to socialize or be involved at all. This will make you become more self-conscious and worried about what others are thinking about you, and if they can see your mistakes. The feeling of helplessness can set in, and your hope of succeeding diminishes, so you give up. You may try again. The cycle repeats, only giving a reinforced gift of failure, that grips your self- confidence deeper each spin. Positive thinking can help you escape.

Positive thinking does not mean that you are ignoring the situation. It just means that you will be more purposeful in thinking positively about it and trying to find a solution. Positive thinking will help you cope and reduce the stress in your life. Think positively about yourself. Be kind to yourself and love yourself. Create a habit of being more optimistic.Be aware of areas that you may feel more negative about, such as work, or health issues, and think of something more positive. Encourage yourself. Stop during the day, and take note of what you are thinking about. Awareness leads to understanding to help your growth. Make it a point to change the negative thought to a positive one. Practice will help with becoming less self critical. Changing how you think will affect your emotional health to believe in yourself.

The third area to be aware of for your success is to **remember where you came from.** Our past is our past. It has helped us become who we are. Not all of our experiences were pleasant, but not all were horrific. We are continually growing and changing. Be thankful for your life and what you have come through. God has been there to help you. By looking back, take strength in seeing that we can learn and make decisions to change our path, if we desire. What we have survived makes us stronger to get past the next challenge in life.

We can't change our past, but we can learn from it. We can grow and become better as a wife, a mother, a friend. Many times we personalize our pain of the things we have had happen to us, and it produces shame and unmerited guilt. We have thoughts to blame ourselves and believe the things were our fault. Let the weights that have kept you from your destiny be left behind, and choose to go forward in this moment. Remember that it was not your fault. You are still very valuable and worthy. You are stronger than you give yourself credit. Affirm yourself every day.

Lastly, **find time for you to get encouragement from others and let them help you with your success.** There is strength in numbers. If you look at a piece of twine or yarn, you will see how the threads are woven together to strengthen it. Surround yourself with positive women. Make sure those who are speaking into your life are uplifting and supportive, so that when you need advice or feedback, you can trust them to give you what you need. A trusted friend can assist with your awareness for you to become more self confident. A friend will not just tell you what you want to hear, but where you need to grow in a loving way.

One of my favorite scriptures is Philippians 4:13. I can do all things through Christ who strengthens me.

What ideas do you have for yourself to become a better woman, friend, wife or mother? Believe in yourself to do it. You are one of a kind, and here for a purpose. You are a gift to those in your world. Don't limit yourself to what you can accomplish. God will not call you to do something to fail. Follow your dreams.

About Sandra Rawlings, MS, LPC, CPCS

Sandra Rawlings is the Director and President of Touch of Healing Counseling and Mental Health Services. Having more than 25 years as a Licensed Professional Counselor in Georgia and Florida, she has experience working with children and adults of all ages. In Florida, she worked for a substance abuse treatment agency, providing counseling and school programs for at-risk children and families. After relocating to Georgia, she has worked in private practice and founded Touch of Healing Counseling Center. She is a Certified Professional Counselor Supervisor, helping those new to the therapy field. Her professional memberships include: the Licensed Professional Counselors Association of Georgia, American Association of Christian Counselors and the International Board of Professional Christian Counselors. This year, she will complete her Certification as a Play Therapist. She loves speaking and has written several articles. Another passion is teaching, as she and her husband have had a Sunday Couple and Family Class for over 15 years.

Tracey Forde

"Your worth is inherent because you are a child of God"

- Tracey Forde

— CHAPTER SEVEN —

Count It All Joy

By Tracey Forde

"Count it all joy, my brothers, when you meet trials of various kinds, for you know that the testing of your faith produces steadfastness. And let steadfastness have its full effect, that you may be perfect and complete, lacking in nothing". - James 1:2–4, ESV

I remember the first time I read this scripture; I was about 10 years old. I couldn't understand how in the world someone could 'count it all joy' when they've lost a loved one, been terminated from their job or broke up with their significant other.

As an adult, I now understand that 'counting it all joy' means tapping into the sacredness in hardships to see that there is purpose in everything that happens to and for us, good & bad.

However, for most of us, when we're going through a situation that cuts us deeply, we can't tap into this mindset unless we've learned how to master our thoughts.

For example, I struggled with emotional abandonment issues from my father. I couldn't 'count it all joy' until I was in my 40s when I wholeheartedly started my healing journey to step into my authentic, unapologetic self.

Over time I was able to intentionally repurpose the hurt and pain of my childhood into wisdom and personal truths. As a result, my capacity to love myself deepened. Additionally, I learned how to intimately and lovingly honor & re-parent my inner child to continue to heal from childhood trauma. This growth is a big part of my legacy of healing to break the traumatic generational cycles of my family while setting my ancestors free and paving a brighter path for my descendants.

Having supported many clients in healing from their traumatic life experiences, in addition to my own trauma, I noticed several actions that empowered us to create & live our best life as we filled the holes in hearts to reclaim our wholeness:

1. **P.U.S.H.**

    - be **P**ersistent!

    - be willing to be **U**ncomfortable!

    - **S**how up for yourself!

    - **H**old yourself accountable!

If you want to understand 'why' you have to have the last word when interacting with others and how it's affecting your life, **P.U.S.H**!

If you want more peace, ease and flow in all areas of your life, **P.U.S.H**!

If you're ready to show up as your authentic self as a parent, in your relationships, at work, everywhere, **P.U.S.H**!

If you want to be happier, more prosperous, stop code switching, throw away your 'masks', stop the hurt, kick fear to the curb, **P.U.S.H**!

You will have to **P.U.S.H.** yourself out of your comfort zone to heal!!

Get started, commit as often as needed daily to **P.U.S.H.** and your breakthroughs will make room for positive changes as you DO THE WORK.

2. Give Yourself Permission to Be Vulnerable.

Vulnerability is an emotion that Black women rarely give themselves permission to feel. Why? We've been told that vulnerability belongs only to white women. Second, we've been conditioned to wear & wholeheartedly uphold the Strong Black Woman trope & the Superwoman schema. Both are proving to be albatrosses around our necks.

Our mental, emotional and physiological futures are dependent on us learning how to be vulnerable to liberate ourselves, decolonize our minds, live our best lives & change the narrative for future generations.

Below are two steps to learn how to be vulnerable:

- Ask for help.
- Allow yourself to feel & lean into your emotions to process the past for what it truly is. This will require vulnerability, honesty and transparency.

3. Accept What you Can't Control and What Has Already Happened

Acceptance is NOT giving in or giving up. It is letting go of what or how we want things to be and learning to see them for what they are and were.

Acceptance gives you permission to lighten your load,

beautiful. Shame, guilt and emotional baggage are heavy burdens to bear!

Acceptance opens the door to joy, peace of mind, love, abundance, gratefulness & forgiveness.

4. Re-Claim Your True Identity

Learn from your mistakes to gain clarity on who you are, what you're capable of & how freakin' awesome you really are!! In other words, tap into who God says you are to unlearn who or what the world says you are.

5. Lighten Your Load.

The longer you hold onto people, situations, circumstances and things that no longer serve you the longer you will be disempowered, unfulfilled and unhappy.

It's time to find the voice you've suppressed to 'keep the peace' to minimize causing additional trauma to yourself.

Muster up the courage to set the necessary boundaries to protect your peace, respect yourself and be treated the way you want & deserve.

Choosing to say 'NO' to allowing trauma to take over your life liberates and empowers you in ways you never imagined possible.

6. Reclaim your Worth.

Your worth is inherent because you are a child of God. It's your internal sense of knowing that you are good enough and worthy of love and belonging.

Sadly, many of us feel unworthy because we grew up with parents & caretakers that didn't realize the harmful impact of their actions (inaction) & words (lack of words).

Some even believed that "sticks & stones may break my bones, but words will never hurt me". They were wrong! Just like physical wounds, verbal wounds hurt & leave scars, too.

I know the abuse & neglect - whether direct or indirect - still stings.

It's up to you if you'll continue to believe that you're unworthy.

Or you can put their words on trial. From there, tap into the TRUTH of who you are to RECLAIM YOUR WORTH.

7. Speak Your Truth.

I was the queen of holding my tongue to keep the peace, to not hurt anyone's feelings, to be the bigger person, to keep the family's name pristine.

What my family forgot to tell me was the weight of holding my tongue on me mentally, physically & emotionally.

Suppressing your truth - aka secrets - and your emotions is too heavy a burden to bear. Not to mention the pressure all that 'weight' is wreaking on your body.

The path to your healing is THROUGH YOUR STORY, beautiful!

Telling your story releases you from shame and guilt while giving you back vulnerability and transparency.

The longer you suppress your truth & your emotions the longer you continue to play small & limit your amazing potential.

The longer you suppress your truth & your emotions you allow trauma to define you and reinforce the limiting beliefs & unhealthy, painful patterns in your life that are not serving you.

The longer you suppress your truth & your emotions the longer it will take for you to BECOME who you truly are!

SPEAK YOUR TRUTH, SIS!

FEEL YOUR EMOTIONS, BEAUTIFUL!

HEAL, SIS, HEAL!

The moment you own your story the lighter the 'weight' on your shoulders & in your spirit.

Second, owning your story liberates you so that it no longer has the power to hurt, cripple, demean or defeat you!

There's one thing I know: wanting and doing are not the same! You can live whole and be empowered when you commit to DOING the work to heal.

About Tracey Forde

Tracey Forde is a wife, mother, entrepreneur and fierce female!

She became a mom at the tender age of 16 and walked into a life of domestic abuse unknowingly at 18 when she married her children's father. After leaving that marriage & marrying again, she realized that she needed to do some serious healing.

So, she walked away from what many would deem the 'good life': great man, beautiful home, luxury cars, good credit. It was the best decision she ever made for herself because it was the beginning of her finding, embracing and accepting herself.

Today, she's a sought after Trauma Healing & Mindset Coach, speaker, writer and businesswoman. Her passion lies in helping Black women achieve success in all areas of their lives, empowering them to live life on their terms and be **#fearlessauthenticunapologetic** as they ***GROW. THRIVE. FLOURISH.***

www.ingramcontent.com/pod-product-compliance
Lightning Source LLC
Chambersburg PA
CBHW071635040426
42452CB00009B/1628